Maryland Crab Cakes

A Delectable Collection of Recipes Celebrating the Chesapeake Bay's Finest Delicacy

While every precaution has been taken in the preparation of this book, the publisher assumes no responsibility for errors or omissions, or for damages resulting from the use of the information contained herein.

MARYLAND CRAB CAKES

First edition. December 2, 2023.

Copyright © 2023 john ahmad.

ISBN: 979-8223171324

Written by john ahmad.

Table of Contents

Maryland Crab Cakes..1

Chapter 1: Introduction to Maryland Crab Cakes 2

Chapter 2: Classic Maryland Crab Cake..................................6

Chapter 3: Chesapeake Bay Inspired Crab Cakes 10

Chapter 4: Mini Crab Cake Bites 14

Chapter 5: Gluten-Free Crab Cakes 18

Chapter 6: Healthy Baked Crab Cakes................................. 23

Chapter 7: Spicy Cajun Crab Cakes................................. 26

Chapter 8: Maryland Crab Cake Sliders 30

Chapter 9: Asian Fusion Crab Cakes 34

Chapter 10: Keto-friendly Crab Cakes................................. 37

Chapter 11: Vegan Crab Cakes 40

Chapter 12: Stuffed Crab Cakes 44

Chapter 13: Crab Cake Benedicts 47

Chapter 14: Crab Cake Tacos................................... 51

Chapter 15: Crab Cake Pasta Delights 54

Chapter 16: Grilled Crab Cakes 59

Chapter 17: Crab Cake Sides and Salads................................. 64

Chapter 18: Creative Crab Cake Garnishes 68

Chapter 19: Crab Cake Leftover Makeovers........................... 71

Chapter 20: Crab Cake Desserts................................... 74

John Ahmad

Chapter 1: Introduction to Maryland Crab Cakes

Maryland Crab Cakes hold a special place in the hearts of seafood lovers worldwide, with their delectable blend of succulent crab meat and flavorful seasonings. In this chapter, we'll delve into the rich history of crab cakes in Maryland, explore the various types of crab meat used, and learn about the essential ingredients and cooking tools that make these cakes a true culinary delight.

1.1 The History of Crab Cakes in Maryland

A Journey Back in Time: Origins and Evolution of Crab Cakes

The story of Maryland Crab Cakes dates back centuries, to the time when Native Americans and early settlers in the Chesapeake Bay region first discovered the abundance of blue crabs. These early inhabitants ingeniously incorporated crab into their diet, using it as a staple source of sustenance.

As time went on, crab recipes evolved, and in the 19th century, the concept of the crab cake as we know it today began to take shape. Local seafood markets and family recipes played a significant role in popularizing crab cakes throughout Maryland and beyond.

Chesapeake Bay's Influence on the Crab Cake Tradition

The Chesapeake Bay, with its nutrient-rich waters, is the lifeblood of the Maryland crabbing industry. The blue crab (Callinectes sapidus) thrives in the bay's brackish waters, making it the primary source of fresh crab meat for these sumptuous cakes. The connection between the Chesapeake Bay's ecosystem and the crab cake's cultural significance is inseparable.

Historical Significance and Cultural Relevance

Maryland Crab Cakes have become more than just a culinary delight; they are now a symbol of the state's heritage and culinary pride. The crabbing and seafood industry have played a crucial role in shaping the culture and identity of Maryland. Many families pass down cherished crab cake recipes through generations, keeping the tradition alive.

1.2 Understanding the Different Types of Crab Meat

Jumbo Lump Crab Meat: Sweet and Meaty Delicacy

Jumbo lump crab meat, the most sought-after and prized variety, consists of large, succulent chunks of white crab meat sourced from the muscle connecting the crab's back swimming legs. This premium crab meat offers a sweet, delicate flavor and an impressive appearance, making it perfect for elegant, high-end crab cakes.

Lump Crab Meat: Ideal for Classic Crab Cakes

Lump crab meat, slightly smaller than jumbo lump, is derived from broken jumbo lumps and smaller pieces of meat. Despite the smaller size, lump crab meat still offers excellent flavor and texture, making it a popular choice for classic Maryland crab cakes.

Backfin Crab Meat: Balancing Cost and Flavor

Backfin crab meat includes a combination of lump and special-grade crab meat from the body cavity of the crab. It offers a good balance between quality and cost, making it a popular choice for those seeking delicious crab cakes without breaking the bank.

Claw Meat: Robust and Flavorful Option

Claw meat, harvested from the crab's claws, is darker and more robust in flavor compared to lump and jumbo lump meat. While it may not be as visually appealing, claw meat adds a unique richness to crab cakes and is a favorite among those who enjoy stronger crab flavor.

Special Considerations: Fresh vs. Pasteurized Crab Meat

When preparing crab cakes, the choice between fresh and pasteurized crab meat can impact the overall taste and texture of the final dish. Fresh crab meat is prized for its natural sweetness and tender texture, but it requires careful handling and must be used quickly. Pasteurized crab meat, on the other hand, has a longer shelf life and is pre-cooked, making it more convenient but may have a slightly different taste and texture.

1.3 Essential Ingredients for Perfect Crab Cakes

Creating the perfect Maryland crab cake is all about balance and showcasing the natural sweetness of the crab meat. While recipes may vary, some ingredients are essential in achieving that delectable flavor and texture:

High-quality crab meat: Opt for fresh or pasteurized crab meat based on availability and preference.

Breadcrumbs: Provide structure and absorb excess moisture while allowing the crab flavor to shine.

Mayonnaise: Binds the ingredients together and adds richness to the crab cake.

Egg: Another binder that helps hold the ingredients together during cooking.

Dijon mustard: Adds a subtle tanginess and depth of flavor to the crab cake.

Worcestershire sauce: Enhances the umami flavor and complements the sweetness of the crab.

Old Bay seasoning: A quintessential blend of spices that gives Maryland crab cakes their signature taste.

Fresh herbs and aromatics: Chopped parsley, chives, and minced garlic provide extra flavor and freshness.

Salt and pepper: Season to taste, ensuring a well-balanced flavor profile.

Cooking Tools for Successful Crab Cakes

To ensure your Maryland crab cakes turn out perfectly, having the right cooking tools is essential:

Mixing bowl: For combining the crab cake ingredients thoroughly without overworking the crab meat.

Rubber spatula: To gently fold the ingredients together, avoiding excessive breaking of the crab meat.

Baking sheet or plate: To shape and chill the crab cake mixture before cooking.

Non-stick skillet or frying pan: For pan-frying the crab cakes to a golden brown and crispy exterior.

Cooking oil or clarified butter: To prevent sticking and achieve a delicious crust when frying.

Mastering the art of making Maryland Crab Cakes involves a deep appreciation for the heritage of this beloved seafood dish and understanding the key elements that contribute to its timeless appeal. Armed with this knowledge, you're ready to embark on a culinary journey that celebrates the Chesapeake Bay's finest delicacy.

Chapter 2: Classic Maryland Crab Cake

A Timeless Recipe with Jumbo Lump Crab Meat

There's something truly magical about a classic Maryland crab cake made with the finest jumbo lump crab meat. The rich sweetness of the crab, paired with the perfect blend of seasonings, creates a culinary masterpiece that captures the essence of the Chesapeake Bay. In this chapter, we'll take you through the steps of crafting this timeless recipe, ensuring that every bite is a celebration of Maryland's culinary heritage.

2.1 The Beauty of Jumbo Lump Crab Meat

Jumbo lump crab meat is the star of the show in this classic crab cake recipe. Derived from the large muscles that connect the crab's back swimming legs, jumbo lump crab meat boasts impressive size and a delicate texture. When using jumbo lump crab meat, it's crucial to handle it with care to preserve its natural sweetness and tenderness. Seek out reputable seafood markets or local crabbers to source the freshest jumbo lump crab meat possible.

2.2 Crafting the Perfect Maryland Crab Cake

Creating the perfect crab cake is an art form that requires attention to detail and a delicate touch. Follow these steps to ensure your crab cakes are a true delight:

Ingredients:

- 1 pound jumbo lump crab meat, carefully picked through for shells
- 1/4 cup mayonnaise
- 1 tablespoon Dijon mustard
- 1 tablespoon Old Bay seasoning
- 1 tablespoon minced fresh parsley
- 1 teaspoon Worcestershire sauce
- Pinch of salt and black pepper to taste
- 1/2 cup breadcrumbs (preferably panko or fresh breadcrumbs)

Instructions:

1. Preparing the Crab Meat:
2. In a large bowl, gently pick through the crab meat to remove any shells or cartilage. Be careful not to break up the large lumps of crab meat.

Mixing the Ingredients:

1. In the same bowl with the crab meat, add the mayonnaise, Dijon mustard, Old Bay seasoning, minced parsley, Worcestershire sauce, salt, and black pepper.
2. Carefully fold the ingredients together using a rubber spatula until well combined. Be gentle to avoid breaking up the jumbo lump crab meat.

Adding the Binders:

Sprinkle the breadcrumbs over the mixture and gently fold them in until the mixture holds together. Avoid overmixing to maintain the crab's texture.

Shaping the Crab Cakes:

Divide the crab mixture into equal portions and shape each portion into a round, flat cake about 3 inches in diameter and 1 inch thick. You can use a ring mold or simply shape them by hand.

2.3 Perfecting the Cooking Method

To achieve the signature golden crust on the outside and a tender, moist interior, the cooking method plays a crucial role. There are two popular methods for cooking Maryland crab cakes: pan-frying and deep-frying.

Pan-Frying:

1. In a large non-stick skillet, heat a couple of tablespoons of vegetable oil or clarified butter over medium heat.
2. Gently place the crab cakes into the skillet and cook for about 3-4 minutes per side, or until they turn golden brown and crispy.
3. Be careful when flipping the crab cakes, as they are delicate. Use a spatula to support them while turning.

Deep-Frying:

1. Heat vegetable oil in a deep fryer or a deep, heavy-bottomed pot to 350°F (175°C).
2. Carefully lower the crab cakes into the hot oil using a slotted spoon or frying basket, and fry them for about 2-3 minutes until they are golden brown and crispy.
3. Remove the crab cakes from the oil and let them drain on a plate lined with paper towels.

2.4 Suggested Serving Accompaniments

A classic Maryland crab cake deserves equally delightful accompaniments to enhance the overall dining experience. Here are some suggestions to complement your crab cakes perfectly:

Remoulade Sauce: A tangy and creamy sauce made with mayonnaise, Dijon mustard, capers, cornichons, and fresh herbs. The bright flavors complement the crab cakes beautifully.

Lemon Wedges: Serve fresh lemon wedges on the side to squeeze over the crab cakes, adding a burst of citrusy brightness.

Fresh Salad: A light and refreshing salad with mixed greens, cherry tomatoes, cucumber, and a simple vinaigrette, providing a crisp contrast to the crab cakes.

Coleslaw: A classic coleslaw with shredded cabbage and carrots, tossed in a creamy dressing, offers a satisfying crunch and creaminess to balance the richness of the crab cakes.

Homemade Potato Chips: Thinly sliced potatoes fried to crispy perfection, serving as a delightful side to the crab cakes.

Cornbread: Soft and crumbly cornbread pairs wonderfully with crab cakes, creating a delightful combination of flavors and textures.

Present your classic Maryland crab cakes with these suggested accompaniments to elevate the dining experience and savor the true taste of the Chesapeake Bay's finest delicacy.

Chapter 3: Chesapeake Bay Inspired Crab Cakes

Adding Local Flavors to Enhance the Taste

The Chesapeake Bay region is not only home to some of the freshest and most delicious crab meat, but it also boasts a rich culinary heritage that has influenced the flavors and ingredients used in traditional crab cake recipes. In this chapter, we will explore how to infuse Chesapeake Bay-inspired flavors into your crab cakes, taking them to new heights of taste and enjoyment.

3.1 Exploring Local Ingredients

The Chesapeake Bay region is known for its abundance of fresh seafood and locally sourced produce. To truly capture the essence of the bay in your crab cakes, consider incorporating some of these signature ingredients:

Sweet Corn: Fresh corn adds natural sweetness and a delightful crunch to the crab cake mixture, enhancing the overall flavor profile.

Chesapeake Bay Blue Crab Seasoning: This locally made seasoning blend complements the Old Bay seasoning and adds a unique Chesapeake Bay twist to your crab cakes.

Fresh Herbs: From chives and tarragon to thyme and cilantro, using locally grown herbs adds brightness and depth to the dish.

Scallions: Adding thinly sliced scallions provides a gentle onion flavor that pairs wonderfully with crab.

3.2 Chesapeake Bay Spice Blend

One of the defining features of Chesapeake Bay cuisine is the iconic spice blend known as Old Bay seasoning. This flavorful blend of spices, including paprika, celery salt, black pepper, and more, has become synonymous with crab cakes and seafood dishes in the region.

Creating your own Chesapeake Bay-inspired spice blend allows you to customize the seasoning to your taste preferences. Experiment with the ratios of the spices to achieve the perfect balance of flavors, and don't be afraid to add a pinch of other complementary herbs and spices to make it your own.

3.3 Adding Sweet and Savory Flavors

The Chesapeake Bay region is celebrated for its juxtaposition of sweet and savory flavors in dishes. To add a delightful interplay of tastes to your crab cakes, consider incorporating the following:

Smoky Bacon: Crispy bacon pieces lend a smoky and savory dimension to the crab cake mixture, enhancing the overall taste experience.

Caramelized Onions: Slow-cooked onions develop a rich sweetness that pairs beautifully with the sweetness of crab meat.

Roasted Garlic: Roasted garlic brings a mellow, nutty flavor that complements the delicate taste of crab.

By combining sweet and savory elements, you can create crab cakes that are a symphony of flavors, perfectly balanced and irresistibly delicious.

3.4 Local Seafood Companions

In addition to crab, the Chesapeake Bay offers a bounty of other delicious seafood options. Incorporating locally caught fish, such as rockfish or striped bass, into your crab cakes can be a delightful addition. By blending different types of seafood, you not only enhance the taste but also pay homage to the region's diverse seafood traditions.

Consider creating a seafood medley crab cake that features a combination of crab meat and other fresh local seafood. The harmonious flavors of the various seafood ingredients will result in a culinary delight that truly celebrates the Chesapeake Bay's seafood-rich heritage.

Regional Variations and Traditions

The Chesapeake Bay region is vast and diverse, and with that comes an array of regional variations and traditions when it comes to crab cake recipes. In this section, we will explore some of the distinct styles of crab cakes found in different areas around the bay, each with its own unique twist.

3.5 Baltimore Style Crab Cakes

Baltimore is known for its love of crab cakes, and the city has its own take on this classic dish. Baltimore-style crab cakes are renowned for their simplicity, focusing on highlighting the flavor of the crab itself. These cakes often feature larger chunks of jumbo lump crab meat and minimal fillers to allow the crab's sweetness to shine through.

To create an authentic Baltimore-style crab cake, select the best quality jumbo lump crab meat and use just enough breadcrumbs and binding agents to hold the cakes together. Season with a light touch of Old Bay seasoning or your Chesapeake Bay-inspired spice blend to enhance the crab's natural taste without overpowering it.

3.6 Eastern Shore Traditions

The Eastern Shore of Maryland holds its own traditions when it comes to crab cakes. Eastern Shore-style crab cakes often feature a balanced combination of crab meat and fillers like breadcrumbs, mayonnaise, and mustard. The use of regional herbs and spices, such as tarragon or Old Bay, is common in these recipes, imparting unique flavors that distinguish them from other variations.

To craft an Eastern Shore-style crab cake, focus on achieving the perfect texture and balance between crab and fillers. Choose the right type of crab meat, as a mix of lump and backfin crab meat can provide an excellent combination of texture and flavor. Experiment with the seasoning to find the ideal ratio that brings out the best in your crab cakes.

By exploring the Chesapeake Bay's local ingredients, spice blends, and regional variations, you can create Chesapeake Bay-inspired crab cakes that celebrate the rich culinary heritage of the region. Whether you choose to embrace Baltimore-style simplicity or Eastern Shore tradition, each variation reflects the essence of the bay and the cherished crab cake traditions that have been passed down for generations.

Chapter 4: Mini Crab Cake Bites

Bite-sized Crab Cakes for Entertaining

Mini crab cake bites are a delightful and elegant addition to any gathering or party. In this chapter, we'll explore how to create these delectable bite-sized treats that are perfect for entertaining guests. From crafting the perfect mini crab cakes to creative presentation ideas, we'll help you impress your guests with these flavorful morsels.

4.1 Crafting Mini Crab Cakes

Creating mini crab cake bites requires a slightly different approach than making traditional-sized crab cakes. Follow these steps to shape and cook these bite-sized gems:

Ingredients:

- 1 pound jumbo lump crab meat, carefully picked through for shells
- 1/4 cup mayonnaise
- 1 tablespoon Dijon mustard
- 1 teaspoon Old Bay seasoning
- 1 tablespoon minced fresh parsley
- 1/2 cup panko breadcrumbs
- 1 large egg, lightly beaten
- 2 tablespoons unsalted butter, melted
- Vegetable oil or clarified butter for frying

Instructions:

Preparing the Crab Meat:

- In a large bowl, gently pick through the crab meat to remove any shells or cartilage. Be careful not to break up the large lumps of crab meat.

Mixing the Ingredients:

- In the same bowl with the crab meat, add the mayonnaise, Dijon mustard, Old Bay seasoning, minced parsley, and half of the panko breadcrumbs.
- Gently fold the ingredients together using a rubber spatula until well combined.

Adding the Binders:

- In a separate small bowl, mix the remaining panko breadcrumbs and melted butter.
- Add the buttered breadcrumbs to the crab mixture and fold them in until the mixture holds together. The buttered breadcrumbs act as a binder and provide a delightful crunch to the mini crab cakes.

Shaping the Mini Crab Cakes:

- Take a tablespoon-sized portion of the crab mixture and gently shape it into a mini crab cake, about 2 inches in diameter and 1/2 inch thick. Repeat with the remaining mixture.

Frying the Mini Crab Cakes:

- In a large non-stick skillet, heat about 1/4 inch of vegetable oil or clarified butter over medium heat.
- Carefully place the mini crab cakes into the skillet and cook for about 2-3 minutes per side, or until they turn golden brown and crispy.
- Use a spatula to carefully flip the mini crab cakes to avoid breaking them.

4.2 Choosing the Right Crab Meat

For mini crab cakes, backfin crab meat is an excellent choice. It offers a combination of white lump crab meat and smaller pieces that work perfectly for bite-sized treats. Alternatively, you can use a mix of jumbo lump and backfin crab meat for an even more luxurious texture.

When handling the crab meat, be gentle to avoid breaking up the lumps. The integrity of the crab meat is essential for creating perfect mini crab cake bites.

4.3 Binders and Fillers for Mini Crab Cakes

In addition to the traditional mayonnaise and Dijon mustard, panko breadcrumbs and melted butter act as the main binders and fillers for mini crab cakes. Panko breadcrumbs provide a light and airy texture, while the melted butter adds richness and enhances the overall flavor.

The balance between the crab meat and the binders is crucial. Use just enough breadcrumbs and binder to hold the crab cakes together without overpowering the crab's taste. The goal is to create bite-sized crab cakes that are tender and moist on the inside, with a crispy exterior.

4.4 Mini Crab Cake Flavor Variations

Mini crab cake bites are incredibly versatile, allowing you to experiment with different flavor variations to suit your guests' preferences. Here are some ideas to get creative with your mini crab cakes:

Spicy Cajun Bites: Add a kick to your mini crab cakes by incorporating Cajun spices, cayenne pepper, and a touch of hot sauce. Serve with a zesty remoulade sauce for a spicy twist.

Asian Fusion Bites: Infuse your crab cakes with Asian flavors by adding minced ginger, soy sauce, and chopped scallions. Serve with a drizzle of sweet chili sauce for an irresistible combination.

Mediterranean Inspired Bites: Mix in chopped roasted red peppers, kalamata olives, and crumbled feta cheese for a Mediterranean twist. Pair these bites with a tangy lemon-garlic aioli.

4.5 Dipping Sauces and Presentation Ideas

Dipping sauces elevate the flavor of mini crab cakes and offer guests the opportunity to customize their bites. Here are some delicious dipping sauce ideas:

Classic Remoulade: A creamy blend of mayonnaise, Dijon mustard, capers, chopped pickles, and fresh herbs.

Lemon-Garlic Aioli: A smooth and zesty aioli made with mayonnaise, minced garlic, lemon juice, and lemon zest.

Sweet Chili Sauce: A slightly sweet and tangy sauce with a touch of heat that complements the crab cake's flavor.

Sriracha Mayo: A spicy and creamy mayo-based sauce with a kick of sriracha for those who enjoy some heat.

Presentation Ideas:

Skewered Bites: Thread mini crab cakes onto small bamboo skewers for a stylish and easy-to-serve presentation.

Mini Serving Spoons: Place mini crab cake bites on individual serving spoons, drizzle with sauce, and garnish with fresh herbs for an elegant appetizer display.

Bite-Sized Sliders: Serve mini crab cake bites between slider buns with lettuce and a dollop of remoulade for a fun and flavorful party treat.

Mini Muffin Tin: Use a mini muffin tin to shape and bake your crab cake bites for a uniform and attractive presentation.

By incorporating different flavors, dipping sauces, and creative presentation ideas, you can create an array of mini crab cake bites that will delight your guests and make your gathering truly unforgettable. Whether served as an appetizer or a party finger food, these bite-sized treats are sure to be a crowd-pleaser.

Chapter 5: Gluten-Free Crab Cakes

Delicious Alternatives for Gluten-Sensitive Diners

For individuals with gluten sensitivities or those following a gluten-free lifestyle, enjoying classic crab cakes can be a challenge. In this chapter, we'll explore how to create mouthwatering gluten-free crab cakes that everyone can savor. From gluten-free binders and fillers to alternative coating options, these crab cakes will be a delightful addition to your repertoire.

5.1 Gluten-Free Binders and Fillers

When crafting gluten-free crab cakes, it's essential to choose appropriate binders and fillers that provide structure and flavor without compromising the gluten-free aspect. We'll introduce you to a variety of gluten-free options that work beautifully in these delectable crab cakes.

Ingredients:

- 1 pound jumbo lump crab meat, carefully picked through for shells
- 1/4 cup gluten-free mayonnaise
- 1 tablespoon Dijon mustard
- 1 teaspoon gluten-free Old Bay seasoning (check for gluten-free label)
- 1 tablespoon minced fresh parsley
- 1/2 cup gluten-free breadcrumbs (see instructions below for making your own)
- 1 large egg, lightly beaten
- 2 tablespoons unsalted butter, melted
- Vegetable oil or clarified butter for frying

Instructions:
Preparing the Crab Meat:

- In a large bowl, gently pick through the crab meat to remove any shells or cartilage. Be careful not to break up the large lumps of crab meat.

Mixing the Ingredients:

- In the same bowl with the crab meat, add the gluten-free mayonnaise, Dijon mustard, gluten-free Old Bay seasoning, minced parsley, and half of the gluten-free breadcrumbs.
- Gently fold the ingredients together using a rubber spatula until well combined.

Adding the Gluten-Free Binders:

- In a separate small bowl, mix the remaining gluten-free breadcrumbs and melted butter.
- Add the buttered breadcrumbs to the crab mixture and fold them in until the mixture holds together. The gluten-free breadcrumbs act as a binder and provide a delightful crunch to the crab cakes.

Shaping the Gluten-Free Crab Cakes:

- Take a tablespoon-sized portion of the crab mixture and gently shape it into a mini crab cake, about 2 inches in diameter and 1/2 inch thick. Repeat with the remaining mixture.

Frying the Gluten-Free Crab Cakes:

- In a large non-stick skillet, heat about 1/4 inch of vegetable oil or clarified butter over medium heat.
- Carefully place the mini crab cakes into the skillet and cook for about 2-3 minutes per side, or until they turn golden brown and crispy.

- Use a spatula to carefully flip the mini crab cakes to avoid breaking them.

5.2 The Role of Gluten-Free Breadcrumbs

Gluten-free breadcrumbs are a key ingredient in creating the perfect texture for crab cakes. Here's how to make your own gluten-free breadcrumbs using various ingredients:

Ingredients:

- Gluten-free bread slices (approximately 4 slices)

Instructions:

1. Preheat the oven to 350°F (175°C).
2. Cut the gluten-free bread into small cubes and spread them out on a baking sheet.
3. Bake the bread cubes in the preheated oven for about 10-15 minutes or until they are dry and crisp. Make sure not to let them brown too much.
4. Once the bread cubes are cooled, transfer them to a food processor or blender.
5. Pulse the bread cubes until they turn into fine breadcrumbs. Be careful not to over-process, as you want a texture similar to regular breadcrumbs.
6. Store the gluten-free breadcrumbs in an airtight container for future use in various recipes.

5.3 Using Nut Flours and Cornmeal

Nut flours and cornmeal are excellent alternatives to traditional wheat-based breadcrumbs. They add a unique nutty flavor and delightful crunch to gluten-free crab cakes. Here's how to incorporate them into your recipe:

Ingredients:

- 1/2 cup almond flour or cornmeal

Instructions:

1. Replace half of the gluten-free breadcrumbs in the crab cake recipe with almond flour or cornmeal.
2. Proceed with the recipe as instructed, combining the nut flour or cornmeal with the gluten-free breadcrumbs and other ingredients.
3. Mix and shape the crab cakes as usual, frying them until golden brown and crispy.

5.4 Incorporating Quinoa and Rice

Quinoa and rice are naturally gluten-free grains that can be used to create an alternative coating for gluten-free crab cakes. Here's how to use quinoa or rice as a crunchy and nutritious coating option:

Ingredients:

- 1 cup cooked quinoa or rice
- 1 large egg, lightly beaten

Instructions:

1. Prepare cooked quinoa or rice according to the package instructions and let it cool slightly.
2. Dip each mini crab cake into the beaten egg, coating it evenly.
3. Press the crab cake into the cooked quinoa or rice, covering the surface completely.
4. Gently pat the quinoa or rice coating onto the crab cake to adhere.
5. Fry the quinoa or rice-coated crab cakes until they turn golden brown and crispy on the outside.
6. Using quinoa or rice as a coating not only adds a delightful texture to the crab cakes but also provides an extra nutritional boost.

By incorporating gluten-free binders and fillers, as well as alternative coating options, you can create flavorful and satisfying gluten-free crab cakes that everyone can enjoy. Whether for a special occasion or a casual gathering, these gluten-free crab cakes are sure to be a hit among all your guests.

Chapter 6: Healthy Baked Crab Cakes

Lightening Up the Classic Recipe

For those seeking a healthier version of the classic crab cake, baking offers a wonderful alternative to frying. In this chapter, we'll explore how to create healthy baked crab cakes that retain all the delicious flavors without the added oil and fat. From choosing the right ingredients to mastering the baking technique, these crab cakes will be a guilt-free delight.

6.1 Healthier Ingredients

To make healthy baked crab cakes, we'll focus on using wholesome and nutrient-rich ingredients while reducing the use of excess fats and fillers. Discover how to create a lighter version of this beloved dish without compromising on taste and texture.

Ingredients:

- 1 pound jumbo lump crab meat, carefully picked through for shells
- 1/4 cup plain Greek yogurt
- 1 tablespoon Dijon mustard
- 1 tablespoon minced fresh parsley
- 1 teaspoon Old Bay seasoning
- 1/2 cup whole wheat breadcrumbs
- 1 large egg, lightly beaten
- 1 tablespoon fresh lemon juice
- 1 tablespoon olive oil
- Pinch of salt and black pepper to taste

Instructions:

Preparing the Crab Meat:

- In a large bowl, gently pick through the crab meat to remove any

shells or cartilage. Be careful not to break up the large lumps of crab meat.

Mixing the Ingredients:

- In the same bowl with the crab meat, add the plain Greek yogurt, Dijon mustard, minced parsley, Old Bay seasoning, and half of the whole wheat breadcrumbs.
- Gently fold the ingredients together using a rubber spatula until well combined.

Adding the Binders:

- In a separate small bowl, whisk together the beaten egg, fresh lemon juice, olive oil, salt, and black pepper.
- Pour the egg mixture into the crab mixture and fold them together until all ingredients are evenly distributed.

Shaping the Crab Cakes:

- Preheat the oven to 375°F (190°C).
- Line a baking sheet with parchment paper or lightly grease it with olive oil.
- Divide the crab mixture into equal portions and shape each portion into a round, flat cake about 2 1/2 inches in diameter and 1/2 inch thick. Place the crab cakes on the prepared baking sheet.

Baking the Crab Cakes:

- Bake the crab cakes in the preheated oven for approximately 12-15 minutes, or until they turn golden brown and are heated through.

6.2 Lightening Up the Binders

In traditional crab cake recipes, mayonnaise and butter are often used as binders. However, to make healthier baked crab cakes, we'll use plain Greek yogurt and a small amount of olive oil as alternatives. These ingredients provide a creamy texture and a touch of richness without the excess fats and calories.

Greek yogurt not only acts as a binder but also adds a tangy flavor that complements the sweetness of the crab. Olive oil helps keep the crab cakes moist and contributes heart-healthy fats.

6.3 Baking Techniques for Perfect Texture

Baking crab cakes requires a slightly different approach to achieve that crispy exterior and moist interior without frying in oil. By preheating the oven and using a baking sheet lined with parchment paper or lightly greased, the crab cakes will cook evenly and develop a lovely golden color.

Baking the crab cakes at a moderate temperature of 375°F (190°C) allows them to cook through without drying out or becoming too browned. Keep a close eye on the crab cakes while baking to ensure they reach the desired level of crispiness.

With these healthier ingredients and baking techniques, you can enjoy the deliciousness of crab cakes without any guilt. Serve these light and flavorful baked crab cakes at your next gathering or as a satisfying weeknight dinner, and savor every bite without worrying about excess fats.

Chapter 7: Spicy Cajun Crab Cakes

A Fiery Twist to the Traditional Recipe

For those who enjoy bold and fiery flavors, Spicy Cajun Crab Cakes offer an exciting variation to the classic recipe. In this chapter, we'll explore how to create crab cakes with a kick, infusing them with the vibrant spices of Cajun cuisine. From selecting the right spices to balancing the heat with delicious flavors, these crab cakes will ignite your taste buds in the most delightful way.

7.1 Embracing Cajun Spices

Cajun cuisine is renowned for its robust and zesty flavors, and in this section, we'll dive into the essential spices that give Spicy Cajun Crab Cakes their fiery twist. Discover the perfect blend of seasonings to bring the authentic taste of the Bayou to your crab cakes.

Ingredients:

- 1 pound jumbo lump crab meat, carefully picked through for shells
- 1/4 cup mayonnaise
- 1 tablespoon Dijon mustard
- 2 tablespoons Cajun seasoning (store-bought or homemade, see instructions below)
- 1 tablespoon fresh lemon juice
- 1/2 cup breadcrumbs
- 1 large egg, lightly beaten
- 2 tablespoons unsalted butter, melted
- Vegetable oil or clarified butter for frying

Instructions:

Preparing the Crab Meat:

- In a large bowl, gently pick through the crab meat to remove any

shells or cartilage. Be careful not to break up the large lumps of crab meat.

Mixing the Ingredients:

- In the same bowl with the crab meat, add the mayonnaise, Dijon mustard, Cajun seasoning, and fresh lemon juice.
- Gently fold the ingredients together using a rubber spatula until well combined.

Adding the Binders:

- In a separate small bowl, mix the breadcrumbs and melted butter.
- Add the buttered breadcrumbs to the crab mixture and fold them in until the mixture holds together. The breadcrumbs act as a binder and provide a delightful crunch to the crab cakes.

Shaping the Spicy Cajun Crab Cakes:

- Take a tablespoon-sized portion of the crab mixture and gently shape it into a mini crab cake, about 2 inches in diameter and 1/2 inch thick. Repeat with the remaining mixture.

Frying the Crab Cakes:

- In a large non-stick skillet, heat about 1/4 inch of vegetable oil or clarified butter over medium heat.
- Carefully place the mini crab cakes into the skillet and cook for about 2-3 minutes per side, or until they turn golden brown and crispy.
- Use a spatula to carefully flip the mini crab cakes to avoid breaking them.

7.2 Balancing Heat with Flavor

Cajun seasoning is the heart of Spicy Cajun Crab Cakes, providing the fiery twist that makes these crab cakes stand out. However, balancing the heat with other delicious flavors is essential to ensure the spices don't overpower the delicate taste of the crab.

Cajun seasoning typically includes a combination of paprika, cayenne pepper, garlic powder, onion powder, thyme, and other spices. The amount of cayenne pepper can vary, depending on how spicy you want your crab cakes to be. Adjusting the level of heat allows you to customize the crab cakes to your taste preference.

To balance the heat, the use of mayonnaise and Dijon mustard in the recipe provides a creamy and tangy counterbalance to the spice. The fresh lemon juice adds brightness and zest, further enhancing the flavor profile.

Serve these Spicy Cajun Crab Cakes with a cooling sauce, such as a creamy remoulade or a refreshing cucumber yogurt dip, to complement the heat and provide a refreshing contrast.

7.3 Homemade Cajun Seasoning

If you prefer to make your own Cajun seasoning, here's a simple recipe to create the fiery blend at home:

Ingredients:

- 2 tablespoons paprika
- 1 tablespoon garlic powder
- 1 tablespoon onion powder
- 1 tablespoon dried thyme
- 1 teaspoon dried oregano
- 1 teaspoon cayenne pepper (adjust to desired level of heat)
- 1 teaspoon black pepper
- 1 teaspoon white pepper
- 1 teaspoon salt

Instructions:

1. In a small bowl, combine all the spices and mix well until evenly distributed.
2. Store the homemade Cajun seasoning in an airtight container in a cool, dry place for future use.

By embracing the bold flavors of Cajun spices and balancing the heat with delightful ingredients, Spicy Cajun Crab Cakes will bring a fiery twist to the traditional recipe. Whether served as a tantalizing appetizer or a mouthwatering main course, these crab cakes are sure to become a favorite among spice enthusiasts and those craving an extra kick in their seafood dishes. Enjoy the Bayou's spirited flavors in every bite!

Chapter 8: Maryland Crab Cake Sliders

Mini Crab Cake Sandwiches with Tasty Toppings

Maryland Crab Cake Sliders offer a delightful way to enjoy the flavors of crab cakes in bite-sized sandwiches. In this chapter, we'll explore how to create these mini delights with an array of delicious toppings. Whether you're hosting a slider party or looking for creative variations, these sliders will be the star of any gathering.

8.1 Crafting Maryland Crab Cake Sliders

Creating Maryland Crab Cake Sliders requires a slightly different approach to shaping and cooking the crab cakes. Discover how to make these mini sandwiches, perfect for serving as appetizers or a fun main course.

Ingredients for Crab Cakes:

- 1 pound jumbo lump crab meat, carefully picked through for shells
- 1/4 cup mayonnaise
- 1 tablespoon Dijon mustard
- 1 teaspoon Old Bay seasoning
- 1 tablespoon minced fresh parsley
- 1/2 cup breadcrumbs
- 1 large egg, lightly beaten
- 2 tablespoons unsalted butter, melted
- Vegetable oil or clarified butter for frying

Ingredients for Sliders:

- Slider buns or mini brioche rolls
- Lettuce leaves (butter lettuce or arugula works well)
- Sliced ripe tomatoes

- Sliced red onions
- Pickles or pickled cucumbers
- Slider sauce (recipe included below)

Instructions for Crab Cakes:
Preparing the Crab Meat:

- In a large bowl, gently pick through the crab meat to remove any shells or cartilage. Be careful not to break up the large lumps of crab meat.

Mixing the Ingredients:

- In the same bowl with the crab meat, add the mayonnaise, Dijon mustard, Old Bay seasoning, minced parsley, and half of the breadcrumbs.
- Gently fold the ingredients together using a rubber spatula until well combined.

Adding the Binders:

- In a separate small bowl, mix the remaining breadcrumbs and melted butter.
- Add the buttered breadcrumbs to the crab mixture and fold them in until the mixture holds together. The breadcrumbs act as a binder and provide a delightful crunch to the crab cakes.

Shaping the Crab Cakes:

- Take a tablespoon-sized portion of the crab mixture and gently shape it into a mini crab cake, about 2 inches in diameter and 1/2 inch thick. Repeat with the remaining mixture.

Frying the Crab Cakes:

- In a large non-stick skillet, heat about 1/4 inch of vegetable oil or clarified butter over medium heat.
- Carefully place the mini crab cakes into the skillet and cook for about 2-3 minutes per side, or until they turn golden brown and crispy.
- Use a spatula to carefully flip the mini crab cakes to avoid breaking them.

Instructions for Slider Sauce:
Ingredients:

- 1/4 cup mayonnaise
- 1 tablespoon Dijon mustard
- 1 tablespoon fresh lemon juice
- 1 tablespoon chopped dill pickles
- 1 teaspoon Old Bay seasoning

Instructions:

1. In a small bowl, whisk together the mayonnaise, Dijon mustard, fresh lemon juice, chopped dill pickles, and Old Bay seasoning until well combined.
2. Taste and adjust seasoning to your preference. Add more Old Bay or lemon juice if desired.
3. Instructions for Assembling the Maryland Crab Cake Sliders:
4. Slice the slider buns or mini brioche rolls in half.
5. Spread a generous amount of slider sauce on the bottom half of each bun.
6. Place a lettuce leaf on top of the sauce.
7. Carefully place a hot mini crab cake on top of the lettuce.
8. Add a slice of ripe tomato, a few slices of red onion, and pickles or pickled cucumbers.

9. Top with the other half of the bun.
10. Secure the sliders with toothpicks if needed and serve immediately.

8.2 Slider Party Ideas and Variations

Maryland Crab Cake Sliders are perfect for a slider-themed party, where guests can enjoy an assortment of mini sandwiches with various toppings and sauces. Here are some slider party ideas and delicious variations to consider:

BBQ Crab Cake Sliders: Top the crab cakes with a dollop of tangy barbecue sauce and a slice of crispy bacon for a smoky and savory twist.

Spicy Sriracha Sliders: Drizzle Sriracha mayo on the crab cakes and add sliced jalapeños or banana peppers for those who enjoy some heat.

Avocado-Lime Sliders: Mash ripe avocado with a squeeze of fresh lime juice and spread it on the buns before adding the crab cakes for a creamy and refreshing option.

Caprese Crab Cake Sliders: Replace the slider sauce with basil pesto and add fresh mozzarella slices and basil leaves for a delightful Italian-inspired variation.

Asian Sesame Sliders: Mix soy sauce, sesame oil, and a touch of honey to create a savory glaze for the crab cakes. Top with sliced cucumbers, pickled ginger, and a sprinkle of toasted sesame seeds.

Offering a variety of toppings and sauces allows guests to customize their Maryland Crab Cake Sliders to suit their taste preferences, making your slider party a memorable and enjoyable experience for all.

Chapter 9: Asian Fusion Crab Cakes

Incorporating Asian Ingredients and Flavors

Asian Fusion Crab Cakes offer a delightful twist to the traditional recipe by infusing the delicate sweetness of crab with the bold and vibrant flavors of Asian cuisine. In this chapter, we'll explore how to create crab cakes that showcase the harmonious combination of soy, ginger, and sesame seeds. Elevate your culinary experience with these mouthwatering crab cakes inspired by the Far East.

9.1 Embracing Asian Flavors

Asian cuisine is known for its balance of flavors, and in this section, we'll dive into the essential ingredients that bring a unique twist to Asian Fusion Crab Cakes. Discover the perfect blend of soy, ginger, and sesame seeds that will transport your taste buds to the captivating tastes of Asia.

Ingredients:

- 1 pound jumbo lump crab meat, carefully picked through for shells
- 1/4 cup mayonnaise
- 1 tablespoon soy sauce (low-sodium recommended)
- 1 tablespoon grated fresh ginger
- 1 tablespoon chopped scallions (green parts)
- 1 tablespoon toasted sesame oil
- 1/2 cup panko breadcrumbs
- 1 large egg, lightly beaten
- 2 tablespoons sesame seeds (white or black)
- Vegetable oil or clarified butter for frying

Instructions:

Preparing the Crab Meat:

- In a large bowl, gently pick through the crab meat to remove any

shells or cartilage. Be careful not to break up the large lumps of crab meat.

Mixing the Ingredients:

- In the same bowl with the crab meat, add the mayonnaise, soy sauce, grated fresh ginger, chopped scallions, and toasted sesame oil.
- Gently fold the ingredients together using a rubber spatula until well combined.

Adding the Binders:

- In a separate small bowl, mix the panko breadcrumbs and sesame seeds.
- Add the breadcrumb and sesame seed mixture to the crab mixture and fold them in until the mixture holds together. The breadcrumbs and sesame seeds act as binders and provide a delightful crunch to the crab cakes.

Shaping the Asian Fusion Crab Cakes:

- Take a tablespoon-sized portion of the crab mixture and gently shape it into a mini crab cake, about 2 inches in diameter and 1/2 inch thick. Repeat with the remaining mixture.

Frying the Crab Cakes:

- In a large non-stick skillet, heat about 1/4 inch of vegetable oil or clarified butter over medium heat.
- Carefully place the mini crab cakes into the skillet and cook for about 2-3 minutes per side, or until they turn golden brown and crispy.
- Use a spatula to carefully flip the mini crab cakes to avoid

breaking them.

9.2 Soy, Ginger, and Sesame Seed Combinations

The magic of Asian Fusion Crab Cakes lies in the combination of soy sauce, fresh ginger, and toasted sesame seeds. Each ingredient contributes its unique flavor profile to create a harmonious blend that perfectly complements the sweetness of the crab.

Soy Sauce: Low-sodium soy sauce enhances the savory umami taste of the crab cakes. Its rich and salty profile brings depth to the dish without overpowering the delicate crab flavor.

Fresh Ginger: Grated fresh ginger adds a zingy and aromatic kick to the crab cakes. The warm and slightly spicy notes of ginger infuse the crab cakes with a burst of freshness.

Toasted Sesame Seeds: The nutty and toasty flavor of sesame seeds provides a delightful crunch to the crab cakes. Toasting the sesame seeds brings out their full aroma, enhancing the overall taste experience.

Toasting the sesame seeds is simple; just heat a dry skillet over medium-low heat and add the sesame seeds. Stir frequently until they turn golden brown and release their fragrance. Be careful not to burn them, as they can become bitter.

By embracing these Asian ingredients and flavors, you can create Asian Fusion Crab Cakes that are a delectable fusion of the Far East and the Atlantic shores. The enticing blend of soy, ginger, and sesame seeds will transport your taste buds to a culinary adventure that marries the best of two culinary worlds.

Chapter 10: Keto-friendly Crab Cakes

Low Carb Options for Crab Cake Lovers

For those following a keto or low-carb lifestyle, enjoying the indulgence of crab cakes can still be a reality. In this chapter, we'll explore how to create keto-friendly crab cakes that are deliciously satisfying without the excess carbs. From choosing the right low-carb ingredients to crafting keto-friendly breadcrumbs and binders, these crab cakes will fit perfectly into your low-carb menu.

10.1 Choosing Low Carb Ingredients

When making keto-friendly crab cakes, it's essential to select ingredients that are low in carbohydrates while still providing the desired texture and flavor. In this section, we'll explore some excellent low-carb options that are perfect for crafting these delightful crab cakes.

Ingredients:

- 1 pound jumbo lump crab meat, carefully picked through for shells
- 1/4 cup mayonnaise (choose a keto-friendly version with no added sugars)
- 1 tablespoon Dijon mustard
- 1 tablespoon minced fresh parsley
- 1 teaspoon Old Bay seasoning (check for any hidden carbs in the brand you choose)
- 1/2 cup almond flour or crushed pork rinds
- 1 large egg, lightly beaten
- 2 tablespoons unsalted butter, melted
- Avocado oil or clarified butter for frying

Instructions:

Preparing the Crab Meat:

- In a large bowl, gently pick through the crab meat to remove any shells or cartilage. Be careful not to break up the large lumps of crab meat.

Mixing the Ingredients:

- In the same bowl with the crab meat, add the mayonnaise, Dijon mustard, minced parsley, and Old Bay seasoning.
- Gently fold the ingredients together using a rubber spatula until well combined.

Choosing Keto-friendly Binders:

- In a low-carb version of crab cakes, traditional breadcrumbs are replaced with keto-friendly alternatives like almond flour or crushed pork rinds. Both options provide a similar breadcrumb-like texture without the excess carbs.

Adding the Low Carb Binders:

- In a separate small bowl, mix the almond flour or crushed pork rinds and melted butter.
- Add the buttered almond flour or pork rinds to the crab mixture and fold them in until the mixture holds together. The keto-friendly binders ensure the crab cakes maintain their shape while adhering to the low-carb aspect.

Shaping the Keto-friendly Crab Cakes:

- Take a tablespoon-sized portion of the crab mixture and gently shape it into a mini crab cake, about 2 inches in diameter and 1/2 inch thick. Repeat with the remaining mixture.

Frying the Crab Cakes:

- In a large non-stick skillet, heat about 1/4 inch of avocado oil or clarified butter over medium heat.
- Carefully place the mini crab cakes into the skillet and cook for about 2-3 minutes per side, or until they turn golden brown and crispy.
- Use a spatula to carefully flip the mini crab cakes to avoid breaking them.

10.2 Keto-friendly Breadcrumbs and Binders

Traditional breadcrumbs are a significant source of carbs in crab cakes, but with a few keto-friendly alternatives, you can achieve the perfect texture without compromising on flavor. Here are two excellent options:

Almond Flour: Almond flour is finely ground blanched almonds and serves as a fantastic low-carb replacement for breadcrumbs. It adds a subtle nutty flavor and provides a tender texture to the crab cakes.

Crushed Pork Rinds: Pork rinds are another fantastic breadcrumb alternative for a keto-friendly version of crab cakes. Crushed pork rinds offer a crispy and savory coating while being virtually carb-free.

Both almond flour and crushed pork rinds can be found in most grocery stores or specialty markets. Choose the one that suits your taste preference and dietary needs best.

By choosing low-carb ingredients and keto-friendly breadcrumbs and binders, you can savor the deliciousness of crab cakes without straying from your low-carb lifestyle. These keto-friendly crab cakes are a delightful addition to your keto menu, making it easy to enjoy the flavors of the sea while staying true to your dietary goals.

Chapter 11: Vegan Crab Cakes

Plant-Based Alternatives to Crab Meat

Vegan Crab Cakes offer a delicious plant-based twist on the classic recipe, perfect for those following a vegan or vegetarian lifestyle. In this chapter, we'll explore how to create mouthwatering vegan crab cakes using plant-based alternatives to crab meat. From crafting tasty vegan sauces and spices to ensuring the right texture, these vegan crab cakes will impress even the most discerning palates.

11.1 Plant-Based Crab Meat Alternatives

When making vegan crab cakes, it's essential to choose the right plant-based alternatives that mimic the taste and texture of crab meat. In this section, we'll explore some fantastic plant-based alternatives that work wonderfully in these delightful vegan crab cakes.

Ingredients:

- 1 pound plant-based crab meat alternative (such as hearts of palm, artichoke hearts, or jackfruit), finely chopped
- 1/4 cup vegan mayonnaise
- 1 tablespoon Dijon mustard
- 1 tablespoon minced fresh parsley
- 1 teaspoon Old Bay seasoning (ensure it's vegan-friendly)
- 1/2 cup breadcrumbs (choose gluten-free breadcrumbs for a gluten-free version)
- 1 large flax egg (1 tablespoon ground flaxseed mixed with 3 tablespoons water)
- 2 tablespoons vegetable oil or vegan butter, melted
- Vegetable oil or vegan butter for frying

Instructions:

Preparing the Plant-Based Crab Meat Alternative:

- Depending on the plant-based crab meat alternative you choose (such as hearts of palm, artichoke hearts, or jackfruit), finely chop or shred it to resemble the texture of crab meat.

Mixing the Ingredients:

- In a large bowl, add the finely chopped plant-based crab meat alternative, vegan mayonnaise, Dijon mustard, minced parsley, and Old Bay seasoning.
- Gently fold the ingredients together using a rubber spatula until well combined.

Crafting Vegan Binders:

- To replace the egg binder in traditional crab cakes, we'll use a flax egg. To make a flax egg, mix 1 tablespoon of ground flaxseed with 3 tablespoons of water. Let it sit for a few minutes until it thickens and becomes gel-like.

Adding the Vegan Binders:

- Add the prepared flax egg to the crab mixture and fold it in until the mixture holds together. The flax egg acts as a binder and helps the vegan crab cakes maintain their shape.

Shaping the Vegan Crab Cakes:

- Take a tablespoon-sized portion of the crab mixture and gently shape it into a mini crab cake, about 2 inches in diameter and 1/2 inch thick. Repeat with the remaining mixture.

Frying the Vegan Crab Cakes:

- In a large non-stick skillet, heat about 1/4 inch of vegetable oil or vegan butter over medium heat.
- Carefully place the mini vegan crab cakes into the skillet and cook for about 2-3 minutes per side, or until they turn golden brown and crispy.
- Use a spatula to carefully flip the mini vegan crab cakes to avoid breaking them.

11.2 Crafting Tasty Vegan Sauces and Spices

Vegan crab cakes can be elevated with the addition of tasty vegan sauces and spices. Here are some delicious options to complement the flavors of these plant-based crab cakes:

Vegan Remoulade: Mix vegan mayonnaise with capers, Dijon mustard, chopped pickles, and a splash of lemon juice to create a tangy and creamy vegan remoulade sauce.

Spicy Chipotle Aioli: Blend vegan mayonnaise with chipotle peppers in adobo sauce, garlic powder, and lime juice for a smoky and spicy aioli that pairs perfectly with the vegan crab cakes.

Tangy Mango Salsa: Combine diced mango, red bell pepper, red onion, cilantro, lime juice, and a pinch of chili powder for a refreshing and tropical salsa topping.

Creamy Avocado Cilantro Sauce: Blend ripe avocado with fresh cilantro, lime juice, garlic, and a dash of cumin to create a creamy and vibrant sauce.

Experiment with different sauces and spices to find the perfect accompaniment to your vegan crab cakes. These delicious plant-based alternatives and flavorful sauces will make these vegan crab cakes a favorite among vegans and non-vegans alike. Enjoy the scrumptious flavors and textures of these plant-based delights at your next gathering or as a delightful weeknight treat!

Chapter 12: Stuffed Crab Cakes

Adding a Delicious Filling to Enhance Texture

Stuffed Crab Cakes take the classic recipe to a whole new level by incorporating a delectable filling inside each crab cake. In this chapter, we'll explore how to create crab cakes with a delightful surprise in the center, elevating the texture and flavor to new heights. Discover creative stuffing combinations that will leave your taste buds longing for more of these mouthwatering stuffed crab cakes.

12.1 Enhancing the Texture with a Filling

The secret to making stuffed crab cakes lies in adding a delicious filling that complements the sweetness and briny flavor of the crab. By incorporating the right filling, you not only enhance the texture but also introduce exciting new taste dimensions to the dish.

Ingredients for Crab Cakes:

- 1 pound jumbo lump crab meat, carefully picked through for shells
- 1/4 cup mayonnaise
- 1 tablespoon Dijon mustard
- 1 teaspoon Old Bay seasoning
- 1 tablespoon minced fresh parsley
- 1/2 cup breadcrumbs
- 1 large egg, lightly beaten
- 2 tablespoons unsalted butter, melted
- Vegetable oil or clarified butter for frying

12.2 Creative Stuffing Combinations

The possibilities for creative stuffing combinations are endless. Let your culinary creativity shine as you experiment with various ingredients to fill the center of these delectable crab cakes. Here are some mouthwatering ideas to get you started:

Creamy Spinach and Artichoke Filling: Mix sautéed spinach, chopped artichoke hearts, vegan cream cheese, and a hint of garlic to create a creamy and savory filling.

Crab and Shrimp Duo: Combine chopped cooked shrimp with the lump crab meat, and season it with a squeeze of fresh lemon juice and a touch of cayenne pepper for a seafood lover's dream.

Boursin Cheese and Sundried Tomatoes: Stuff the crab cakes with a blend of Boursin cheese and chopped sundried tomatoes for a rich and flavorful stuffing.

Corn and Roasted Red Pepper: Add sweetness and color to the center of the crab cakes by mixing roasted corn kernels and diced roasted red pepper with the crab meat.

Avocado and Mango Salsa: Create a tropical twist by stuffing the crab cakes with diced avocado and mango salsa for a refreshing and tangy surprise.

Instructions for Making Stuffed Crab Cakes:
Preparing the Crab Mixture:

- In a large bowl, gently pick through the crab meat to remove any shells or cartilage. Be careful not to break up the large lumps of crab meat.
- Add the mayonnaise, Dijon mustard, Old Bay seasoning, minced parsley, and half of the breadcrumbs to the crab meat.
- Gently fold the ingredients together using a rubber spatula until well combined.

Crafting the Filling:

- Choose your desired filling combination and prepare it separately in a separate bowl.

Shaping the Stuffed Crab Cakes:

- Take a tablespoon-sized portion of the crab mixture and flatten it into a small disc on your palm.
- Place a teaspoonful of your chosen filling in the center of the crab mixture.

Sealing the Stuffed Crab Cakes:

- Carefully fold the edges of the crab mixture over the filling to encase it entirely. Gently shape the stuffed crab cake into a round, flat shape, ensuring the filling remains in the center.

Frying the Stuffed Crab Cakes:

- In a large non-stick skillet, heat about 1/4 inch of vegetable oil or clarified butter over medium heat.
- Carefully place the stuffed crab cakes into the skillet and cook for about 2-3 minutes per side, or until they turn golden brown and crispy.
- Use a spatula to carefully flip the stuffed crab cakes to avoid breaking them.

By adding a delightful filling to the center of the crab cakes, you'll surprise your guests and yourself with the wonderful texture and flavor combination. The creative stuffing combinations will allow you to customize these stuffed crab cakes to your heart's desire, ensuring a delightful culinary experience that will keep everyone coming back for more. Enjoy these stuffed crab cakes as an impressive appetizer at parties or as a gourmet treat for special occasions!

Chapter 13: Crab Cake Benedicts

Elevating Breakfast with Crab Cakes

Crab Cake Benedicts bring a touch of elegance to your breakfast table by combining the richness of crab cakes with the classic indulgence of Eggs Benedict. In this chapter, we'll explore how to create a delightful breakfast dish that is sure to impress your taste buds and guests. Elevate your mornings with the luscious combination of crab cakes, poached eggs, and velvety hollandaise sauce.

13.1 The Perfect Breakfast Fusion

Combining the flavors of crab cakes with the classic elements of Eggs Benedict creates a harmonious fusion that tantalizes the taste buds. The sweet and savory notes of the crab cakes complement the richness of the poached eggs and the velvety hollandaise sauce, resulting in a breakfast dish that is both comforting and indulgent.

Ingredients for Crab Cakes:

- 1 pound jumbo lump crab meat, carefully picked through for shells
- 1/4 cup mayonnaise
- 1 tablespoon Dijon mustard
- 1 teaspoon Old Bay seasoning
- 1 tablespoon minced fresh parsley
- 1/2 cup breadcrumbs
- 1 large egg, lightly beaten
- 2 tablespoons unsalted butter, melted
- Vegetable oil or clarified butter for frying

13.2 Delicious Hollandaise and Egg Variations

The key to a perfect Crab Cake Benedict lies in the hollandaise sauce and egg preparation. Here are some delectable hollandaise and egg variations to elevate your breakfast experience:

Classic Hollandaise Sauce: Create the traditional hollandaise sauce by whisking together egg yolks, lemon juice, and melted butter over a double boiler until thick and creamy. Season with a pinch of cayenne pepper and salt for a classic and luxurious sauce.

Lemon Dill Hollandaise: Add a refreshing twist to the hollandaise sauce by incorporating fresh dill and a generous squeeze of lemon juice. The bright flavors of lemon and dill beautifully complement the crab cakes.

Avocado Hollandaise: For a creamy and vibrant hollandaise, blend ripe avocado with lemon juice, melted vegan butter, and a touch of garlic. The avocado hollandaise adds a healthy twist to the classic sauce.

Egg Variations:

Poached Eggs: Poached eggs are the classic choice for Eggs Benedict. To poach eggs, bring water to a gentle simmer, add a splash of vinegar, and carefully slide in the cracked eggs. Cook for about 3-4 minutes until the whites are set, but the yolks remain runny.

Soft-Boiled Eggs: Soft-boiled eggs with a runny yolk offer an alternative to poached eggs for Crab Cake Benedicts. Cook the eggs in boiling water for about 5-6 minutes, then cool them under cold water before peeling.

Scrambled Eggs: For a twist on tradition, scramble the eggs until light and fluffy. The creamy texture of scrambled eggs pairs wonderfully with the crab cakes and hollandaise sauce.

Instructions for Crab Cake Benedicts:

Prepare the Crab Cakes:

- Follow the instructions provided in the previous chapters (Chapter 3) to create the crab cakes. Set them aside and keep warm while preparing the hollandaise and eggs.

Prepare the Hollandaise Sauce:

- Choose your preferred hollandaise variation from the suggestions provided (Classic Hollandaise, Lemon Dill Hollandaise, or Avocado Hollandaise).
- Keep the hollandaise warm in a double boiler or a heatproof bowl set over a pan of warm water.

Prepare the Eggs:

- Choose your preferred egg variation (Poached Eggs, Soft-Boiled Eggs, or Scrambled Eggs) and prepare them accordingly.

Assembling the Crab Cake Benedicts:

- Place a warm crab cake on each serving plate.
- Top each crab cake with your chosen egg variation (poached, soft-boiled, or scrambled).
- Generously drizzle the hollandaise sauce over the eggs and crab cakes.

Garnish and Serve:

- Garnish the Crab Cake Benedicts with a sprinkle of chopped fresh parsley, a dash of paprika, or a twist of lemon zest for a burst of color and flavor.
- Serve immediately and enjoy the luscious combination of crab cakes, eggs, and hollandaise.

Crab Cake Benedicts are a delightful breakfast indulgence that will make any morning feel like a special occasion. With the rich flavors of the crab cakes, the velvety hollandaise sauce, and the perfectly prepared eggs, this breakfast dish is a wonderful way to start the day with a touch of luxury and elegance. Serve them for a leisurely weekend brunch or as a treat for family and friends on special occasions. Bon appétit!

Chapter 14: Crab Cake Tacos

A Fusion of Seafood and Mexican Cuisine

Crab Cake Tacos bring the flavors of the sea together with the vibrant and spicy notes of Mexican cuisine. In this chapter, we'll explore how to create a mouthwatering fusion dish that combines the best of both worlds. From crafting delicious crab cake fillings to pairing them with fresh salsa and guacamole, these tacos will take your taste buds on a delightful culinary journey.

14.1 Crafting Delicious Crab Cake Fillings

The beauty of Crab Cake Tacos lies in the versatile fillings you can create. From zesty and spicy to creamy and savory, the options are endless. Let's dive into some delectable crab cake fillings that will make your tacos truly unforgettable.

Ingredients for Crab Cakes (optional, from Chapter 3):

- 1 pound jumbo lump crab meat, carefully picked through for shells
- 1/4 cup mayonnaise
- 1 tablespoon Dijon mustard
- 1 teaspoon Old Bay seasoning
- 1 tablespoon minced fresh parsley
- 1/2 cup breadcrumbs
- 1 large egg, lightly beaten
- 2 tablespoons unsalted butter, melted
- Vegetable oil or clarified butter for frying

14.2 Fresh Salsa and Guacamole Pairings

To complete the Crab Cake Tacos experience, serve them with refreshing salsa and creamy guacamole. These toppings add a burst of freshness and flavor that perfectly complements the crab cakes.

Ingredients for Fresh Salsa:

- 2 ripe tomatoes, diced
- 1/2 red onion, finely chopped
- 1 jalapeño, seeds removed and finely chopped
- 1/4 cup fresh cilantro, chopped
- 1 tablespoon fresh lime juice
- Salt and pepper to taste

Instructions for Fresh Salsa:

1. In a bowl, combine the diced tomatoes, chopped red onion, jalapeño, and fresh cilantro.
2. Drizzle the fresh lime juice over the mixture and toss everything together until well combined.
3. Season with salt and pepper to taste. Refrigerate until ready to serve.

Ingredients for Guacamole:

- 2 ripe avocados, peeled and pitted
- 1/4 cup red onion, finely chopped
- 1 small jalapeño, seeds removed and finely chopped
- 2 tablespoons fresh cilantro, chopped
- 1 tablespoon fresh lime juice
- Salt and pepper to taste

Instructions for Guacamole:

1. In a bowl, mash the avocados with a fork until desired consistency is reached.
2. Stir in the chopped red onion, jalapeño, fresh cilantro, and lime juice.
3. Season with salt and pepper to taste. Cover the guacamole with plastic wrap, ensuring it touches the surface to prevent browning. Refrigerate until ready to serve.

Instructions for Crab Cake Tacos:
Prepare the Crab Cakes:

- Follow the instructions provided in Chapter 3 to create the crab cakes. Keep them warm in a low oven while you prepare the toppings.

Warm the Tortillas:

- Heat corn tortillas on a dry skillet over medium heat for a few seconds on each side until they are soft and pliable. Keep them warm in a clean kitchen towel.

Assemble the Tacos:

- Place a warm crab cake in the center of each tortilla.
- Top with a generous spoonful of fresh salsa and a dollop of guacamole.
- Serve and Enjoy:

1. Serve the Crab Cake Tacos immediately with extra fresh salsa and guacamole on the side for those who want to add more toppings.
2. Enjoy the fusion of seafood and Mexican flavors in every delicious bite!

Crab Cake Tacos are a delightful combination of the sea's bounty and the bold flavors of Mexican cuisine. With the mouthwatering crab cake fillings and the fresh salsa and guacamole toppings, these tacos are perfect for a fun and flavorful meal with family and friends. Serve them at your next taco night or fiesta, and watch everyone enjoy the unique and delicious blend of tastes in each taco. Buen provecho!

Chapter 15: Crab Cake Pasta Delights

Crab Cakes as a Pasta Topping or Filling

Crab Cake Pasta Delights combine the richness of crab cakes with the comforting appeal of pasta dishes. In this chapter, we'll explore how to use crab cakes as a delightful topping or filling for various pasta recipes. From creamy Alfredo sauce to zesty marinara options, these pasta dishes will be a true delight for seafood and pasta lovers alike.

15.1 Crab Cake Pasta Topping

Adding crab cakes as a savory topping to pasta dishes introduces a burst of flavor and texture that takes your meal to a whole new level. Let's explore a delectable pasta recipe with crab cakes as the star topping.

Ingredients for Crab Cakes (optional, from Chapter 3):

- 1 pound jumbo lump crab meat, carefully picked through for shells
- 1/4 cup mayonnaise
- 1 tablespoon Dijon mustard
- 1 teaspoon Old Bay seasoning
- 1 tablespoon minced fresh parsley
- 1/2 cup breadcrumbs
- 1 large egg, lightly beaten
- 2 tablespoons unsalted butter, melted
- Vegetable oil or clarified butter for frying

Ingredients for Crab Cake Pasta Topping:

- Cooked pasta of your choice (linguine, fettuccine, or penne work well)
- Your favorite Alfredo sauce (store-bought or homemade)
- Grated Parmesan cheese for garnish
- Fresh parsley or basil leaves for garnish

Instructions for Crab Cake Pasta Topping:
Prepare the Crab Cakes:

- Follow the instructions provided in Chapter 3 to create the crab cakes. Keep them warm in a low oven while you prepare the pasta and sauce.

Cook the Pasta:

- Cook the pasta according to the package instructions until al dente. Drain the pasta, reserving a small amount of pasta water.

Warm the Alfredo Sauce:

- In a separate saucepan, warm the Alfredo sauce over low heat. If the sauce is too thick, add a splash of the reserved pasta water to reach your desired consistency.

Assemble the Crab Cake Pasta Topping:

- Place a serving of cooked pasta on a plate or in a pasta bowl.
- Top the pasta with a warm crab cake.

Drizzle with Alfredo Sauce:

- Generously drizzle the warm Alfredo sauce over the crab cake and pasta.

Garnish and Serve:

- Sprinkle grated Parmesan cheese over the top, and garnish with fresh parsley or basil leaves for a pop of color and added flavor.
- Serve immediately and enjoy the delectable combination of

crab cakes and creamy Alfredo sauce over pasta.

15.2 Crab Cake Stuffed Pasta

Using crab cakes as a filling for stuffed pasta dishes introduces a luxurious and flavorful twist to classic recipes. Let's explore a stuffed pasta recipe that incorporates mouthwatering crab cake filling.

Ingredients for Crab Cakes (optional, from Chapter 3):

- 1 pound jumbo lump crab meat, carefully picked through for shells
- 1/4 cup mayonnaise
- 1 tablespoon Dijon mustard
- 1 teaspoon Old Bay seasoning
- 1 tablespoon minced fresh parsley
- 1/2 cup breadcrumbs
- 1 large egg, lightly beaten
- 2 tablespoons unsalted butter, melted
- Vegetable oil or clarified butter for frying

Ingredients for Crab Cake Stuffed Pasta:

- Jumbo pasta shells or large manicotti tubes
- Your favorite marinara sauce (store-bought or homemade)
- Shredded mozzarella or Parmesan cheese for topping
- Fresh basil leaves for garnish

Instructions for Crab Cake Stuffed Pasta:
Prepare the Crab Cakes:

- Follow the instructions provided in Chapter 3 to create the crab cakes. Set them aside and keep warm while you prepare the pasta and sauce.

Cook the Pasta Shells:

- Cook the jumbo pasta shells or manicotti tubes according to the package instructions until al dente. Drain the pasta and set aside.

Prepare the Marinara Sauce:

- Warm your favorite marinara sauce in a separate saucepan over low heat.

Stuff the Pasta:

- Carefully stuff each cooked pasta shell or manicotti tube with the warm crab cake filling. Be generous with the filling, ensuring each pasta piece is well-filled.

Arrange the Stuffed Pasta in a Baking Dish:

- Preheat your oven to 375°F (190°C).
- Place the stuffed pasta in a baking dish and pour the warm marinara sauce over the top.

Top with Cheese:

- Sprinkle shredded mozzarella or Parmesan cheese over the top of the stuffed pasta.

Bake and Serve:

- Cover the baking dish with foil and bake in the preheated oven for about 15-20 minutes, or until the cheese is melted and bubbly.
- Remove from the oven and let it rest for a few minutes.
- Garnish with fresh basil leaves before serving.

Crab Cake Pasta Delights bring the indulgence of crab cakes to the comfort of pasta dishes. Whether as a savory topping with creamy Alfredo sauce or a luxurious filling in stuffed pasta, these recipes are perfect for special occasions or weeknight dinners when you crave a little something extra. Enjoy the delightful combination of crab cakes and pasta, and savor the rich flavors and textures that this fusion brings to your plate.

Chapter 16: Grilled Crab Cakes

Infusing Smoky Flavors on the Grill

Grilled Crab Cakes take the classic dish to a whole new level by infusing smoky flavors that add depth and complexity. In this chapter, we'll explore how to grill crab cakes using both cedar plank and charcoal grill techniques. Get ready to experience the irresistible smokiness that elevates these crab cakes to a new level of deliciousness.

16.1 Grilling Crab Cakes on Cedar Planks

Grilling crab cakes on cedar planks imparts a smoky aroma and a hint of woody flavor to the delicate crab meat. The natural oils in the cedar wood infuse the crab cakes with a distinctive taste that enhances the overall experience.

Ingredients for Cedar Plank Grilled Crab Cakes:

- 1 pound jumbo lump crab meat, carefully picked through for shells
- 1/4 cup mayonnaise
- 1 tablespoon Dijon mustard
- 1 teaspoon Old Bay seasoning
- 1 tablespoon minced fresh parsley
- 1/2 cup breadcrumbs
- 1 large egg, lightly beaten
- 2 tablespoons unsalted butter, melted
- Cedar planks (food-grade and presoaked in water for at least 1 hour)
- Vegetable oil or clarified butter for brushing

Instructions for Cedar Plank Grilled Crab Cakes:
Prepare the Cedar Planks:

- Before grilling, soak the cedar planks in water for at least 1 hour to prevent them from burning during the cooking process.

Prepare the Crab Cakes:

- Follow the instructions provided in Chapter 3 to create the crab cakes.

Preheat the Grill:

- Preheat your grill to medium-high heat (around 400°F or 204°C).

Grill the Crab Cakes on Cedar Planks:

- Lightly brush the pre-soaked cedar planks with vegetable oil or clarified butter to prevent sticking.
- Place the crab cakes on the cedar planks, leaving some space between them.

Grill with Indirect Heat:

- Place the cedar planks with the crab cakes on the grill, positioning them away from direct heat.

- Close the grill lid and let the crab cakes cook with indirect heat, allowing the smoky cedar flavors to infuse into the crab meat. Grill for about 10-12 minutes or until the crab cakes are cooked through and have a slightly golden crust.

Serve and Enjoy:

- Carefully remove the cedar planks with the grilled crab cakes from the grill.
- Serve the smoky grilled crab cakes with your favorite accompaniments, such as a squeeze of lemon or a dollop of tartar sauce.

16.2 Grilling Crab Cakes on Charcoal Grill

Grilling crab cakes on a charcoal grill imparts a robust smokiness that complements the delicate flavors of the crab meat. The high heat and open flames lend a charred crust to the crab cakes, creating a tantalizing contrast in taste and texture.

Ingredients for Charcoal Grill Grilled Crab Cakes:

- 1 pound jumbo lump crab meat, carefully picked through for shells
- 1/4 cup mayonnaise
- 1 tablespoon Dijon mustard
- 1 teaspoon Old Bay seasoning
- 1 tablespoon minced fresh parsley
- 1/2 cup breadcrumbs
- 1 large egg, lightly beaten
- 2 tablespoons unsalted butter, melted

- Lump charcoal
- Charcoal chimney or lighter fluid for lighting the charcoal
- Vegetable oil or clarified butter for brushing

Instructions for Charcoal Grill Grilled Crab Cakes:
Prepare the Crab Cakes:

- Follow the instructions provided in Chapter 3 to create the crab cakes.

Light the Charcoal Grill:

- Fill a charcoal chimney with lump charcoal and light it using either newspaper or lighter cubes.
- Let the charcoal burn until it develops a layer of gray ash on top.

Set Up the Grill for Direct Heat:

- Once the charcoal has turned to embers, distribute it evenly across the bottom of the grill for direct heat cooking.

Grill the Crab Cakes:

- Lightly brush the grill grates with vegetable oil or clarified butter to prevent sticking.
- Place the crab cakes directly on the grill grates over the hot charcoal.

Grill with Direct Heat:

- Cook the crab cakes on each side for about 2-3 minutes or until they develop a golden crust and are cooked through.

Serve and Enjoy:

- Carefully remove the grilled crab cakes from the grill.
- Serve the char-grilled crab cakes with your favorite accompaniments, such as a drizzle of melted butter or a zesty aioli.

Grilled Crab Cakes are a delightful treat that marries the sweetness of crab with the smokiness of the grill. Whether you choose the cedar plank or charcoal grill technique, these grilled crab cakes will leave your taste buds longing for more of that irresistible smoky flavor. Serve them as a show-stopping appetizer or as the star of your seafood feast for a memorable dining experience. Enjoy the scrumptious fusion of smoky goodness and delicate crab meat in every delicious bite!

Chapter 17: Crab Cake Sides and Salads

Complementing Crab Cakes with Fresh Greens

Crab Cake Sides and Salads add a refreshing and nutritious touch to your crab cake meals. In this chapter, we'll explore various side dishes and salad options that pair perfectly with crab cakes. From classic coleslaw and Caesar salad to creative alternatives, these dishes will complete your crab cake feast.

17.1 Classic Coleslaw

Ingredients for Classic Coleslaw:

- 4 cups shredded green cabbage
- 1 cup shredded carrots
- 1/2 cup mayonnaise
- 2 tablespoons apple cider vinegar
- 1 tablespoon granulated sugar
- 1 teaspoon Dijon mustard
- Salt and pepper to taste

Instructions for Classic Coleslaw:

1. In a large bowl, combine the shredded green cabbage and shredded carrots.
2. In a separate smaller bowl, whisk together the mayonnaise, apple cider vinegar, granulated sugar, Dijon mustard, salt, and pepper until well combined.
3. Pour the dressing over the cabbage and carrots, and toss until the vegetables are evenly coated.
4. Cover the coleslaw with plastic wrap and refrigerate for at least 1 hour before serving to allow the flavors to meld.
5. Serve the classic coleslaw as a cool and crunchy side dish with your crab cakes.

17.2 Caesar Salad with a Twist
Ingredients for Caesar Salad with a Twist:

- 1 large head of romaine lettuce, washed and chopped
- 1 cup croutons (store-bought or homemade)
- 1/2 cup shaved Parmesan cheese
- Caesar dressing (store-bought or homemade)
- Grilled shrimp or prawns (optional, for added protein)

Instructions for Caesar Salad with a Twist:

1. In a large salad bowl, combine the chopped romaine lettuce and croutons.
2. Drizzle the desired amount of Caesar dressing over the lettuce and croutons, and toss until everything is well coated.
3. Add the shaved Parmesan cheese to the salad and gently toss again.
4. For an extra special touch, top the Caesar salad with grilled shrimp or prawns to complement the crab cakes with additional seafood flavors.
5. Serve the Caesar salad with a twist alongside your crab cakes for a satisfying and flavorful combination.

17.3 Fresh Spinach and Berry Salad
Ingredients for Fresh Spinach and Berry Salad:

- 6 cups fresh baby spinach leaves
- 1 cup fresh strawberries, hulled and sliced
- 1/2 cup fresh blueberries
- 1/4 cup chopped pecans or walnuts
- Goat cheese crumbles (optional, for added creaminess)
- Balsamic vinaigrette dressing (store-bought or homemade)

Instructions for Fresh Spinach and Berry Salad:

1. In a large salad bowl, combine the baby spinach leaves, sliced strawberries, fresh blueberries, and chopped pecans or walnuts.
2. If desired, add some goat cheese crumbles to the salad for a creamy and tangy element that complements the sweetness of the berries.
3. Drizzle the desired amount of balsamic vinaigrette dressing over the salad, and gently toss until all the ingredients are coated.
4. Serve the fresh spinach and berry salad as a vibrant and nutritious side dish that complements the flavors of your crab cakes.

17.4 Mediterranean Orzo Salad
Ingredients for Mediterranean Orzo Salad:

- 1 cup orzo pasta, cooked and cooled
- 1/2 cup cherry tomatoes, halved
- 1/2 cup cucumber, diced
- 1/4 cup Kalamata olives, pitted and sliced
- 1/4 cup crumbled feta cheese
- 2 tablespoons chopped fresh parsley
- 2 tablespoons extra-virgin olive oil
- 1 tablespoon red wine vinegar
- Salt and pepper to taste

Instructions for Mediterranean Orzo Salad:

1. In a large bowl, combine the cooked and cooled orzo pasta with the cherry tomatoes, cucumber, Kalamata olives, crumbled feta cheese, and chopped fresh parsley.
2. In a small bowl, whisk together the extra-virgin olive oil and red wine vinegar. Season with salt and pepper to taste.
3. Drizzle the dressing over the orzo salad, and toss until all the

ingredients are well combined and coated with the dressing.

4. Serve the Mediterranean orzo salad as a hearty and flavorful side dish that complements the crab cakes with Mediterranean-inspired flavors.

Crab Cake Sides and Salads offer a variety of options to round out your crab cake meals. Whether you prefer the classic coleslaw, a refreshing Caesar salad with a twist, a nutritious spinach and berry salad, or a hearty Mediterranean orzo salad, these dishes will enhance the overall dining experience and provide a delightful contrast to the flavors and textures of the crab cakes. Enjoy the harmonious blend of seafood and fresh greens for a satisfying and well-balanced meal.

Chapter 18: Creative Crab Cake Garnishes

Elevating Presentation with Beautiful Touches

Creative Crab Cake Garnishes add a touch of elegance and beauty to your dishes, making them even more enticing to the eyes and palate. In this chapter, we'll explore how to elevate the presentation of your crab cakes with edible flowers and microgreens. These artistic touches will turn your crab cake creations into stunning and delightful culinary masterpieces.

18.1 Edible Flowers

Edible flowers not only add visual appeal to your crab cakes but also introduce unique flavors that complement the seafood. When using edible flowers, it's essential to ensure they are safe for consumption and have not been treated with harmful chemicals. Here are some edible flowers that work beautifully as crab cake garnishes:

Nasturtium: With its vibrant colors and peppery taste, nasturtium flowers add a pop of flavor and beauty to your crab cakes.

Viola/Pansy: These delicate flowers come in a range of colors and have a mild, slightly sweet flavor that pairs well with seafood.

Chive Blossoms: Chive blossoms have a subtle onion flavor that harmonizes with the savory notes of crab cakes.

Borage: Borage flowers have a mild cucumber flavor that adds a refreshing twist to your dish.

Instructions for Using Edible Flowers as Garnishes:

1. Ensure the flowers are edible and have not been treated with any harmful substances.
2. Gently rinse the flowers with cool water and pat them dry with a paper towel.
3. Carefully arrange the edible flowers on the plate around or on top of the crab cakes.

4. For an extra touch of elegance, scatter a few petals over the dish.
5. Edible flowers not only enhance the presentation but can also be enjoyed with each bite, adding subtle floral notes to the dish.

18.2 Microgreens

Microgreens are young, tender greens that come in various flavors, colors, and textures. These tiny greens are packed with nutrients and add a burst of freshness to your crab cakes. Here are some microgreens that pair wonderfully with crab cakes:

Micro Arugula: Adds a peppery kick that complements the sweetness of the crab.

Micro Basil: Offers a delicate basil flavor that complements the crab cake's savory notes.

Micro Cilantro: Introduces a fresh, citrusy flavor that enhances the overall dish.

Micro Mustard Greens: Adds a slightly spicy and earthy touch to the crab cakes.

Instructions for Using Microgreens as Garnishes:

Rinse the microgreens with cool water and gently pat them dry with a paper towel.

Sprinkle the microgreens over the crab cakes, creating a beautiful and colorful contrast.

Microgreens not only add a visually appealing touch but also provide a delightful burst of flavor and texture.

18.3 The Art of Garnishing

When garnishing your crab cakes with edible flowers and microgreens, consider the overall presentation and aim for a harmonious arrangement. Here are some tips to help you master the art of garnishing:

Create Balance: Arrange the garnishes in a way that balances the colors and shapes on the plate. A symmetrical arrangement or a natural scattering can both work beautifully.

Play with Colors: Use a variety of colorful edible flowers and microgreens to add vibrancy and life to your crab cakes.

Keep it Simple: Garnishes should enhance the dish without overwhelming it. A few well-placed flowers and microgreens can make a big impact.

Be Creative: Don't be afraid to experiment and have fun with the garnishes. Mix and match different flowers and microgreens to create your unique presentation.

Timing: Add the garnishes just before serving to ensure they look fresh and vibrant.

By incorporating creative crab cake garnishes, you can turn a simple dish into a stunning culinary masterpiece. Edible flowers and microgreens not only enhance the visual appeal of your crab cakes but also introduce new flavors that complement the seafood. Embrace your creativity and artistic flair, and watch as your crab cakes take on a new level of sophistication and charm. Enjoy the delightful combination of art and culinary pleasure with these creative crab cake garnishes!

Chapter 19: Crab Cake Leftover Makeovers

Transforming Extra Crab Cakes into New Dishes

Crab Cake Leftover Makeovers offer creative ways to repurpose extra crab cakes into exciting new dishes for breakfast, lunch, and dinner. In this chapter, we'll explore ideas to give your leftover crab cakes a delicious and satisfying makeover, ensuring that no crab cake goes to waste.

19.1 Breakfast: Crab Cake Benedict Breakfast Sandwich

Ingredients for Crab Cake Benedict Breakfast Sandwich:

- Leftover crab cakes
- English muffins or brioche buns
- Poached or fried eggs
- Hollandaise sauce (store-bought or homemade)
- Fresh baby spinach leaves

Instructions for Crab Cake Benedict Breakfast Sandwich:

1. Reheat the leftover crab cakes in the oven or a skillet until they are warm and crisp.
2. Toast the English muffins or brioche buns.
3. Place a warm crab cake on the bottom half of each muffin or bun.
4. Top the crab cakes with a poached or fried egg.
5. Generously drizzle hollandaise sauce over the eggs and crab cakes.
6. Add a handful of fresh baby spinach leaves on top.
7. Place the other half of the muffin or bun on top to complete the sandwich.
8. Serve the Crab Cake Benedict Breakfast Sandwich as a decadent and satisfying morning treat.

19.2 Lunch: Crab Cake Avocado Salad
Ingredients for Crab Cake Avocado Salad:

- Leftover crab cakes
- Ripe avocados, sliced
- Mixed salad greens (e.g., spinach, arugula, or mesclun)
- Cherry tomatoes, halved
- Cucumber, sliced
- Red onion, thinly sliced
- Lemon vinaigrette dressing (store-bought or homemade)

Instructions for Crab Cake Avocado Salad:

1. Reheat the leftover crab cakes in the oven or a skillet until they are warm and crispy.
2. Arrange the mixed salad greens on a serving platter or individual plates.
3. Top the greens with sliced avocado, cherry tomatoes, cucumber, and red onion.
4. Place a warm crab cake on each salad.
5. Drizzle the lemon vinaigrette dressing over the salad.
6. Serve the Crab Cake Avocado Salad as a refreshing and nutritious lunch option.

19.3 Dinner: Crab Cake Pasta Alfredo
Ingredients for Crab Cake Pasta Alfredo:

- Leftover crab cakes, crumbled
- Cooked fettuccine or linguine pasta
- Alfredo sauce (store-bought or homemade)
- Grated Parmesan cheese
- Freshly ground black pepper

- Fresh parsley, chopped

Instructions for Crab Cake Pasta Alfredo:

1. In a saucepan, warm the Alfredo sauce over low heat.
2. Add the crumbled leftover crab cakes to the sauce, and gently heat until they are warmed through.
3. Toss the cooked pasta in the Alfredo sauce and crab cake mixture until well coated.
4. Serve the Crab Cake Pasta Alfredo with a sprinkle of grated Parmesan cheese, freshly ground black pepper, and chopped fresh parsley.
5. Enjoy a rich and indulgent dinner with this delicious crab cake pasta creation.

Crab Cake Leftover Makeovers allow you to enjoy the goodness of crab cakes in new and exciting ways. Whether you're starting the day with a Crab Cake Benedict Breakfast Sandwich, savoring a refreshing Crab Cake Avocado Salad for lunch, or indulging in a comforting Crab Cake Pasta Alfredo for dinner, these makeovers ensure that your leftover crab cakes don't go to waste. Embrace the versatility of crab cakes and turn them into delightful meals for any time of the day.

Chapter 20: Crab Cake Desserts

Unique Sweet Treats Featuring Crab Cakes

Crab Cake Desserts offer a surprising and delightful twist on traditional sweet treats. In this chapter, we'll explore unique dessert ideas that incorporate crab cakes, as well as innovative dessert pairings that complement the flavors of the crab cakes. Get ready to indulge in the unexpected world of crab cake sweets!

20.1 Crab Cake Cheesecake Bites

Ingredients for Crab Cake Cheesecake Bites:

- Leftover crab cakes, crumbled
- Graham cracker crumbs
- Cream cheese
- Sweetened condensed milk
- Lemon juice
- Vanilla extract
- Fresh berries (e.g., strawberries or blueberries) for garnish

Instructions for Crab Cake Cheesecake Bites:

1. Preheat your oven to 350°F (175°C).
2. In a mixing bowl, combine the crumbled leftover crab cakes and graham cracker crumbs to create the crust mixture.
3. Press the crab cake and graham cracker crust mixture into the bottom of mini cupcake liners or a mini muffin pan.
4. In a separate bowl, beat the cream cheese until smooth and creamy.
5. Gradually add the sweetened condensed milk, lemon juice, and vanilla extract to the cream cheese, mixing until well combined.
6. Spoon the cream cheese mixture over the crab cake crusts in the cupcake liners or muffin pan.

7. Bake the crab cake cheesecake bites in the preheated oven for about 15-18 minutes or until the cheesecake is set.

8. Let the cheesecake bites cool to room temperature, then refrigerate until chilled and ready to serve.

9. Garnish each cheesecake bite with fresh berries for a burst of color and added sweetness.

10. Enjoy these unique and scrumptious Crab Cake Cheesecake Bites as a surprising dessert treat!

20.2 Dessert Pairing: Crab Cake Ice Cream Sundae
Ingredients for Crab Cake Ice Cream Sundae:

- Leftover crab cakes, crumbled
- Vanilla ice cream
- Caramel sauce or butterscotch sauce
- Chopped toasted pecans or walnuts
- Whipped cream
- Maraschino cherries for garnish

Instructions for Crab Cake Ice Cream Sundae:

1. Reheat the crumbled leftover crab cakes in the oven or a skillet until they are warm and crispy.

2. In a serving dish, place a scoop of vanilla ice cream.

3. Sprinkle the warm crab cake crumbles over the ice cream.

4. Drizzle caramel sauce or butterscotch sauce over the crab cakes.

5. Add a generous handful of chopped toasted pecans or walnuts.

6. Top with a dollop of whipped cream and a maraschino cherry for a classic sundae finish.

7. Serve the Crab Cake Ice Cream Sundae as a delightful and unexpected dessert pairing.

20.3 Dessert Pairing: Crab Cake Tropical Parfait
Ingredients for Crab Cake Tropical Parfait:

- Leftover crab cakes, crumbled
- Coconut milk yogurt or regular yogurt
- Fresh mango, diced
- Fresh pineapple, diced
- Toasted coconut flakes
- Honey or maple syrup for drizzling
- Fresh mint leaves for garnish

Instructions for Crab Cake Tropical Parfait:

1. Reheat the crumbled leftover crab cakes in the oven or a skillet until they are warm and crispy.
2. In a tall glass or dessert dish, layer coconut milk yogurt or regular yogurt with the warm crab cake crumbles.
3. Add a layer of diced fresh mango and diced fresh pineapple on top of the crab cakes.
4. Sprinkle toasted coconut flakes over the fruit.
5. Drizzle honey or maple syrup over the parfait for added sweetness.
6. Garnish with fresh mint leaves for a tropical touch.
7. Serve the Crab Cake Tropical Parfait as a refreshing and unique dessert pairing.

Crab Cake Desserts open up a world of unexpected and delightful culinary adventures. From the surprising Crab Cake Cheesecake Bites to the innovative dessert pairings like Crab Cake Ice Cream Sundae and Crab Cake Tropical Parfait, these sweet treats will leave your taste buds intrigued and satisfied. Embrace the creativity in combining savory and sweet flavors, and enjoy the delightful fusion of flavors in these unique crab cake desserts and dessert pairings. Indulge yourself in a whole new world of culinary delights!

In this cookbook, we have explored the world of Maryland Crab Cakes and beyond, celebrating the versatility and deliciousness of this iconic seafood dish. From classic Maryland Crab Cakes to creative variations and innovative pairings, we have covered a wide range of recipes and culinary adventures.

The journey began with an introduction to the history of Crab Cakes in Maryland, understanding the different types of crab meat, and essential ingredients and cooking tools to create the perfect crab cake.

We delved into classic Maryland Crab Cake recipes, learning how to make jumbo lump crab meat shine and achieve the right consistency for a truly timeless dish. We also explored Chesapeake Bay-inspired Crab Cakes, adding local flavors and regional variations to elevate the taste.

For those seeking bite-sized delights, Mini Crab Cake Bites offered a perfect option for entertaining, along with delectable dipping sauces and presentation ideas. We accommodated gluten-sensitive diners with Gluten-Free Crab Cakes, exploring alternatives for binders and fillers without sacrificing flavor.

In our quest for healthier options, we discovered the world of Healthy Baked Crab Cakes, mastering the techniques of baking over frying. For those craving a spicy kick, Spicy Cajun Crab Cakes brought the heat while still balancing with flavors.

We didn't forget about the dietary preferences of vegan diners, crafting delicious Vegan Crab Cakes with plant-based alternatives to crab meat and savory vegan sauces and spices. Stuffed Crab Cakes introduced us to creative fillings that elevated the texture of the dish.

Taking the culinary adventure further, we explored Crab Cake Benedicts, Crab Cake Tacos, and Crab Cake Pasta Delights, combining the flavors of crab cakes with various cuisines and dishes, offering a diverse array of delightful options.

And it didn't stop there! We ventured into the realm of grilled goodness with Grilled Crab Cakes, infusing smoky flavors using cedar plank and charcoal grill techniques. We also explored the art of presentation with Creative Crab Cake Garnishes, incorporating edible flowers and microgreens to elevate the visual appeal.

Crab Cake Leftover Makeovers provided clever ways to transform extra crab cakes into new dishes, offering unique breakfast, lunch, and dinner ideas. To our surprise, Crab Cake Desserts showed us that this seafood delicacy could also delight our sweet tooth, with unique treats like Crab Cake Cheesecake Bites and innovative dessert pairings.

In conclusion, this cookbook celebrates the culinary versatility of Maryland Crab Cakes and showcases how this iconic seafood dish can be adapted, elevated, and paired to create a wide range of delightful meals and experiences. Whether you're a seafood enthusiast, a home cook looking to impress, or a food lover seeking unique flavors, these recipes offer something for everyone.

We hope you embark on your culinary journey with these recipes, embracing the creativity and joy of cooking. So, fire up your kitchen, gather your ingredients, and prepare to savor the delicious world of Maryland Crab Cakes and beyond. Enjoy the culinary adventure, and may your dishes be a delight to share and savor with your loved ones. Happy cooking! Bon appétit!